IN THE GARDEN
UNEARTHLY DELIGHTS
THE PAINTINGS OF
JOSH KIRBY

IN THE GARDEN OF UNEARTHLY DELIGHTS

THE PAINTINGS OF JOSH KIRBY

NIGEL SUCKLING

Paper Tiger
A Dragon's World Ltd Imprint
Limpsfield
Surrey RH8 0DY
Great Britain

© 1991 Dragon's World Ltd
© 1991 Illustrations Josh Kirby
© 1991 Text Nigel Suckling
© 1991 Foreword Brian Aldiss
Reprinted 1992

The catalogue record for this book is available from the British Library.

ISBN 1 85028 154 8 (Limpback)

EDITOR Michael Downey
ART DIRECTOR Dave Allen
EDITORIAL DIRECTOR Pippa Rubinstein

Typeset by Dragon's World Ltd
Printed in Singapore

FACING TITLE PAGE

**LORD VALENTINE AND CARABELLA WITH
DELIAMBER THE VROON**

Private work, 1982. After doing a cover for Robert Silverberg's Lord
Valentine's Castle Kirby carried on painting various of the themes suggested
by the book. This is one of about three or four. Another depicts Carabella
and Deliamber mounted on Valentine's horse amongst a multitude of
mercenaries and camp followers, later used as the cover for the second
Silverberg trilogy.

OPPOSITE PAGE

THE MAJIPOOR CHRONICLES

Cover for book by Robert Silverberg, Pan Books, 1983. This picture began as
a private work but was chosen anyway for the sequel to Valentine's Castle.
Because illustration is Kirby's 'work' as well as his employment he often does
more than is strictly necessary. The commissions are his themes so he will
explore and improvise upon them as much as possible just for the fun of it.

CONTENTS

FOREWORD

ruce Sterling said, memorably, that the colour of science fiction is noir. That obviously doesn't apply to Josh Kirby. His colour is surely yellow ogre.

The man's a giant painter. In my study, in serried ranks, stand serious books on Time, most of them admittedly by Dr J. T. Fraser, the world's first chronosopher. I've long sought for some scientific explanation of Time, that weird fluid in which we are all temporarily embalmed. But the imagination is a perverse creature not always prone – indeed often erect in the case of fantasy writers – to scientific regulation. Perhaps that's why I tend to see Time personified as one of Kirby's giants.

Time, then, is a bloated creature, clad only in a furlined loin cloth, probably purloined at that. He's the colour of last year's goat's cheese. He is over-weight, has cholesterol problems, and probably suffers from Hernia, the messenger of the gods with winged scandals. His lumpy face and bulging forehead show clear signs of foetal origin. He's ugly as Sin – some might say, as Virtue.

Such ogres, under Kirby's brush, fall victim to gorgeous damsels. These melon-bottomed nymphets despatch Time easily. In real life, alas, Time eventually despatches all damsels: one reason for treating reality with contempt.

However, Time does occasionally trip itself up and take a tumble. For this is my chance to say how much I admire Kirby's work. I have been waiting for it for about – sorry, Josh! – thirty-five years.

Thirty-five years ago, Kirby and I were both beginning our long and unlikely careers. I was then getting published in a long-vanished magazine, *Authentic*. Covers were by Kirby. I particularly admired his cover for Issue #81. And then – his cover for Issue #82 (July 1957)! It illustrated one of my stories, 'What Triumphs', later incorporated into *Galaxies Like Grains of Sand*. Of course I had no say in this matter. When my complimentary copy of *Authentic* arrived in the post, I was taken by surprise. My first cover.... (My first novel had not then been published.) It was a great event.

Another surprise the following month. I received *Authentic* Issue #83 and there Kirby had presented the world with another cover based on a story of mine ('Out of Reach'). I had arrived.... Or at least was pulling out of the station.

I still have those magazines. There one sees latent all of his later skills. The space dogfight on #82 was daring and individual for its time. The interlocking galactic fleets hurtle at one another like beetles bound for a quick reproductive session, the coleoptera of the spaceways. Kirby is already turning indifferent metal into living forms.

But it's the cover for #83 which remains one of my all-time favourites. It features not coleoptera but a Cleopatra. A raven-haired beauty in a scanty gown makes her way through an hallucinatory maze, followed by a tiger. Around her are walls of flowers and fish. Our bathukolpian beauty looks suitably amazed by all this. It's an intriguing, fantastic, delicate picture, and guaranteed to bring in the customers.

So here we are again. This time I'm covering for Kirby, as it were. But there is little to say that is not conveyed by the pictures here on display. How do we define his art, in which human kind, god- or goblin-like, rides a quasi-religious streak? He's the very best of the humorous fantasy artists. Engraved though his name may be on my heart – or at least my forearm – I'm convinced Kirby is less famous than he should be.

This may be because so often his art has been used on inferior works of fiction – praise be that he and Terry Pratchett have found each other: a marriage made in Heaviside Layers or thereabouts! But another reason may be sought.

To work for paperback publishers is to be employed in a version of Tin Pan Alley; a lot of rush orders are needed, and most of them must conform generically. But Kirby lives in Diss, Norfolk (where the Aldisses came from) and is of an independent frame of mind. 'My Rambo leaps are a millimetre long', he says. I like that remark. It has a resonance, is full of quiet doggedness and defiance. Art for him remains a pleasure, an exploration – not an attitude of which people in publishing houses always approve.

I have to admit I like the way this man lives, in a rotting rectory, painting in what was the butler's pantry. It's right! It figures! That's what his art is all about. The Jabberwocky Universe. Rage, or at least a paddy, in Heaven. Full of jocular jock-strapped figures, crumbling buildings, impossible postures, on-rushing revelation, and moth-eaten mythologies.

These wondrous eomorphs represent the unsuitable in pursuit of the inscrutable. British Chaos is come again – in leaps a millimetre long. To whom else could the Monty Python team have turned for their monster mock-Bruegel, *The Life of Brian*? You can only marvel at Kirby's Tower of Bauble. Architecture in art, St Thomas Aquinas is reported to have quipped, is the slaying of banal fact by beautiful high-as-a-kite hypothesis.

Incidentally, I see the name of Bruegel, and his inheritance, cropping up more than once in these pages. Well, there was more than one Bruegel. Perhaps there's more than one Kirby: that would account for the bubblingly anarchic energy we encounter here. How many personnae are sitting there in Diss, in the rectified rectory?

Let's look again at that little pubescent witch riding a frog on page 82. It's such a kirbyesque image; amusing, grotesque, just mildly threatening, though the woman's on top. She has the creature on a rein. But how long will this elfin creature reign – for the frog is really a prince of the blood?... You tell me. This is the essence of Kirby's pixillated art: we're in for a shock. A pleasant one, of course. Unlike the frog, we ain't going to croak. This is a life-enhancing art.

'Fighting for your life sometimes, that's what art feels like,' says Josh Kirby, looking up momentarily from his crowded drawing-board.

But what we feel like, as viewers of the end result, is life renewed. Great stuff, Josh. For me, you'll always be the Authentic artist.

Brian Aldiss, 1991

INTRODUCTION

Josh Kirby lives in a 'rambling' 400-year old rectory in a small village near Diss in Norfolk, a village which sadly has lost all amenities save a garage and village hall – the pub having disappeared shortly after Kirby's arrival in the mid 1960s, the only shop some years later. Exactly how many years would take some working out, exact chronology not being a Kirby speciality. For this reason the picture dating occasionally needs to be taken with a pinch of salt – intelligent guessing being what it is.

In this isolated and unfocussed community the Rectory is further cut off by being tucked away down a side lane that rather grandly bears its name. Does he mind this isolation? Not at all: 'My main concern always is to be left in peace to pursue my painting, which I mostly do seven days a week. At weekends a lady friend comes to stay, but otherwise I'm here all on my own.'

Although the rectory contains a modern-looking, glass-panelled studio (a recent accomplishment), most of Kirby's painting is still carried out in a little cubbyhole downstairs – 'my cupboard' he calls it, which is not far from the truth as it was once the butler's pantry. There he works on a board wedged unconfidently between paper-crammed shelves and the only narrow window to catch the light (he hates working by artificial light).

Kirby himself is friendly man of indeterminate age. It comes as a slight shock to learn that he was a schoolboy in Liverpool when that city was bombed in the last world war and has vivid memories of huddling under the stairs while bombs blew and searchlights and ack-ack guns raked the sky. Then the next morning collecting shrapnel amid the devastated streets. It was about this time (though any connection is unclear) that he first aspired to be an artist. Soon his school was evacuated to a mining valley in the Black Mountains of south Wales. There Kirby lived with a coal miner's family in a tiny cottage on the banks of the Tawe, which flowed black twice a day when the coal dust was sluiced.

Back in Liverpool after the war he left school for the City Art School, where John Lennon was to make his mark a few years later. There he spent six 'gallivanting' years, soon gaining a precocious reputation as a portrait painter in the grand, formal manner. When his time was up, Kirby went to London to seek his fortune but was recalled in 1950 to paint a portrait of the Lord Mayor of Liverpool, the youngest painter ever thus commissioned by the city and one of a line which includes the illustrious Augustus John.

This was all very well, a flying start any portrait painter might give an arm and a leg for. The only trouble was that Kirby did not particularly enjoy formal portrait painting. There was all the travelling for one thing and the formality itself seemed a cramp on the imagination. What he wanted was something in the same line which did not require having to leave the studio – the closest he could find to this on returning to London was work in a commercial art studio specializing in film posters.

After a few years of this he went freelance, producing covers for a fairly indiscriminate range of subjects – romance, westerns, spy thrillers, war stories – anything that came to hand really. Science fiction was at first no more than another category but slowly the Kirby imagination woke to the potential of the genre and it came to occupy more and more of his time and energy.

The basic problem for Josh Kirby in the 1950s was how to combine earning a living with what he most wanted to do – painting. For him there was not the gulf many see between fine art and illustration, no high principles at stake. 'Was Bruegel a fine artist or illustrator?' he asks. 'And does it matter?' Through his film posters and portraits Kirby started with a foot in both camps. Neither felt quite like home but illustration seemed the lesser evil when it came to specializing.

'The trouble with fine art' he says, 'is that not many people actually make a living from it. Only a few very famous ones and some perhaps who paint landscapes because they are uncontroversial and lots of people want one for the living room wall. Other than landscapes there are not many areas to survive in and I don't find them challenging. Most fine artists I know support themselves by teaching, which was the last thing I ever wanted to do. If you're a fine artist you have maybe one show a year. What do you do if it's raining and no-one comes?'

At one time painters like Bosch and Bruegel were supported by rich patrons or the Church, but there is no equivalent nowadays. Not many buyers can afford to pay good prices for paintings, not enough to support the whole community of artists. In the absence of any other, paperback publishers became Kirby's patrons.

This did not mean entirely abandoning his fine art aspirations all at once. For a while half his time was spent at the easel producing what he now rather wryly calls 'modern' paintings which he tried hawking round the galleries with no great success. Gradually these dried up as the two strands of his output merged to the point where he now rarely feels any distinction between his private work and professional commissions. It is all just painting to him, which is what he set out to do in the first place. It helps that he need do no 'pot-boilers' and can choose his commissions.

Does he have any hints for would-be artists and illustrators on how to achieve this happy condition? 'Not really, I'm afraid. Looking back on my career it seems little more than a series of lucky accidents – being in the right place and meeting the right people at the right time. Frightening really.' From a brief spell in Paris chasing *la vie bohème* and working as a freelance illustrator of film posters Kirby was lured back to

London by the offer of a spacious studio in Bushey. Here he took to spending half his week producing large, flamboyant canvases in the tradition of Picasso and Matisse. The other half was spent painting book covers and smaller easel paintings in the studio of his Battersea house, a converted pickle shop whose large windows let in abundant light. This occupied a quiet little backwater just across the river from Chelsea where he spent the evenings with artist and writer friends. By this time the 1960s were in full swing so it was not all that surprising that Nell Dunn should write *Up the Junction* in an upper room of Kirby's house. At the time everyone was full of ideas and confidence.

By the mid 1960s however, Kirby was married to a country girl from Long Melford in Suffolk who was unhappy about the idea of living in Battersea so they moved to within striking distance of her home. Did he have any regrets about leaving London? 'No real regrets. We missed our friends, naturally, but soon they all began moving out as well.'

Over the years, Kirby's paintings have occasionally been exhibited in galleries, maintaining some link with the world of fine art which he believes is fantasy's ultimate home. Prominent among them are the Institute of Contemporary Art (ICA) and Portal galleries in London. He also held a major exhibition in Berlin in 1986 and a retrospective one-man show in Liverpool in 1988. Other recognitions include being voted Best Professional Artist at the science fiction World Convention in Brighton in 1979. This led to his *Voyage of the Ayeguy* portfolio, of which more will be said later.

On the whole, Kirby does not part with his work easily. Although never denying the necessity of money, it never feels an adequate exchange for a painting, being in itself such a soulless and indiscriminate commodity. However, his work has been sought after by various enthusiasts with a measure of success. Among them is 'Mr Science Fiction', Forrest J. Ackerman, whose famed collection of memorabilia is destined for a purpose-built museum in Los Angeles and contains many Josh Kirby originals. Also Ray Bradbury, whose private collection includes Kirby's covers for *The Illustrated Man* and *Something Wicked This Way Comes* among others.

Over the years he has continued to produce film posters of all kinds, but science fiction became dominant here too. Recent examples are the posters for *Return of the Jedi*, *The Beastmaster*, *Krull*, *Seven Cities to Atlantis*, *Starflight One* and the comedy *Morons from Outer Space*. Also the Monty Python team commissioned a spoof of Bruegel's Tower of Babel for their *Life of Brian*.

In the Garden of Unearthly Delights, the title of this book, is explained by Kirby as, 'an echo of Hieronymous Bosch's *Garden of Earthly Delights*. I like to feel I pass on a torch along with the multitudes of fantasy artists inspired by Bosch and Bruegel. Bruegel took up the torch over 400 years ago, and the light of the imagination set in motion then still guides artists today.'

'"Unearthly" refers to the locationless quality of anything that arises from the world of the imagination. By the power of imagination laws of nature can be upturned, earth sent spinning out of orbit, then returned to stability in the flicker of an eye. We need no longer be glued by our feet to the surface of the planet. We can people worlds as yet undreamed of. The paintings are wrought and crafted on this planet earth. The only contact with this world is paint and canvas. The only evidence is the work – proof that such worlds exist even if only in the imagination.'

THE LIFE OF BRIAN

Film poster, 1979. Used by kind permission of Monty Python. In the end this design was not used for the poster because it contains too many incidents cut from the film at the last moment before release (with some reason, says Kirby, because some were outrageously offensive). It did, however, appear in the book accompanying the film, which was some consolation for the immense amount of labour that went into it.

CHAPTER ONE

VAPOURS OF FORGOTTEN WORLDS

Josh Kirby's name is currently associated most readily with humour. But that is only one aspect of his work which happens to be riding the crest of a wave because of his covers for Terry Pratchett's enormously successful *Discworld* novels. He enjoys humour, naturally, or else the results would look forced, but would hate to find himself suddenly pigeonholed as a humourist and unable to paint anything else.

There is no great danger of this, partly because his skill in other areas is well proven, partly because the genres of fantasy and science fiction are remarkable for their distinct lack of humour. Recent trends aside, how many humourists are there? Before Terry Pratchett there was Douglas Adams, obviously, but otherwise just the odd funny book or character springs to mind. In the 1970s and early 1980s Kirby painted a number of covers for an American science fiction humourist, Ron Goulart, but as far as he knows the books were only published in the US so they cannot claim to have taken the world by storm.

Some might say that science fiction and fantasy in general take themselves altogether too seriously, given that their scenarios are all more or less completely make-believe. But that is to miss the point that, although the scenarios are imaginary, the forces at play are just as real as in any other genre, they are only clothed differently. The thing about fantasy is that it goes straight for the archetypes – forget all that secondary manifestation stuff, let's see what the things look like. It appeals to an area of the imagination once nourished by living cultural myths and legends, which were generally rather lacking in humour too, if you come to think of it. It satisfies a partly spiritual hunger which, as with any other, cannot be understood by those who have never experienced it.

While it would be pretentious to suggest that fantasy always rises to the level of the ancient collective myths, it does its best in a secular age where all the old gods and demons have been largely discredited. For Kirby, science fiction and fantasy painting is: 'A doorway of the mind and through it is not escape from the workaday world but enrichment of it, extension to it, expansion of all one's subtle essences and potentialities. It is a way of life, of thought, an area in which one can explore and experiment with possibilities whose existence might not even be hinted at in the contemporary dark night of the soul.'

Broadly speaking, science fiction explores the future; fantasy explores, well, not exactly the past but it takes us to dimensions where much that has been banished into the dead past lives again, where good and evil are not mere moral judgements over which one can argue but living entities who lead armies to war. In the endless forests of fantasy all our hopes and fears, dreams and phobias walk or skulk abroad in the flesh instead of invisibly crowding the mind.

Josh Kirby's own view of his work is that it is art pure and simple, no matter what definition others may give it. And the role of an artist in society? 'To fulfil a spiritual need, whether the art be serious or light-hearted. Although in a way I don't know what I am doing at all, beyond following an intuitive line which to me seems important. To me, art is like the lungs of society – vital but not obvious. It feels important but it is hard to define exactly, beyond saying that it is a mark of civilization as opposed to brute survival. Without flourishing art, culture crumbles.' Currently, he feels, art tends to be valued more in terms of its market price than any intrinsic worth.

However, given a streak of mulish obstinacy and a complete deafness to good common sense, it is still possible for an artist to carve a comfortable niche in the world and Kirby has no complaints about his. 'The great thing about fantasy and science fiction is that they are a wild free-for-all. Anything goes, philosophy, science, religion, whatever. Personally I'm happier with fantasy than strict science fiction because I am a bit uncomfortable with coldly functional spaceships and other hardware. I like interesting shapes which need a little magic to make them work. That's what I really like in the end – magic. So that anything becomes possible.'

FANTAROT DECK – TWO OF CUPS

Commissioned by a Los Angeles fan, Bruce Pelz, for a set of tarot cards, each by a different artist, 1978. 'Everyone in science fiction' Kirby says, including some amateurs. Why he chose the two of cups he cannot remember but supposes there was only a limited range left at the time.

DUELMASTER II – BLOOD VALLEY

Role playing game cover, 1985. Kirby: 'Heroes rescue heroines in distress – all very exciting to illustrate but the books are awkward to read consecutively as they direct the reader backwards and forwards to follow alternative outcomes. However, they are full of the stuff of fantasy characters and creatures.'

DARYA OF THE BRONZE AGE

Cover for book by Lin Carter, DAW Books, 1981. One of a series of tales set in a vast underground realm where pretty much anything goes.

THE RED CIRCLE

Cover for a role playing game book by
Steven Moskowitz, Corgi, 1986. This was
Kirby's interpretation of a scene from Terry
Pratchett's *The Colour of Magic* (see page 103
for the cover illustration). Initially he painted it
for his own amusement, but it fitted the
events in Moskowitz's book so well that he
used it for this title. Decaying wizards are
quite a common breed in these games!

SAVAGE SCORPIO

Cover for book by Alan Burt Akers, DAW Books, 1978. The
Scorpio series was published by DAW Books, a company founded
in America by a former editor of Ace Books, Donald A. Wollheim,
who took Kirby with him when he left to form DAW Books. The
connection is, Kirby feels, another example of the 'lucky break'
syndrome which is the hallmark of his career. It only came about
because Wollheim happened to attend an exhibition of science
fiction art at the Portal Gallery in London where he found some of
Kirby's paintings and liked them enough to buy one and contact him
with offers of work for Ace.

CAPTIVE SCORPIO
Cover for book by Alan Burt Akers, DAW Books, 1978. The first
of a series of novels which appealed to Kirby because of their pure
fantasy and happy contempt for practical possibility.

WARRIOR OF SCORPIO

Cover for book by Alan Burt Akers, DAW Books, 1975. Kirby:
'Fantastic creatures, warriors and princesses; swashbuckling stuff that
you can get your teeth into! Lots of pug-uglies and primitive
warriors living the barbarian life, rich and flamboyant.'

OPPOSITE PAGE
**JOURNEY TO THE
UNDERGROUND WORLD**

Cover for book by Lin Carter,
DAW Books, 1979. The
characters topple down an
extinct volcano, deeper and
deeper to vast caverns with
oceans and skies self-
illuminated. Here life goes on,
unaware of the long-forgotten
surface hundreds of miles
above. 'All exciting stuff to
paint,' says Kirby.

SUNS OF SCORPIO

Cover for book by Alan Burt
Akers, DAW Books, 1976. Each
of the *Scorpio* books was given
to Kirby as the manuscript was
finished in the later titles. To
save on airmail costs the covers
were painted almost the same
size as they appeared on the
book. This was a rather
restrictive practice which he
would not consider now but at
the time he acquired such a
taste for it that he did the same
with his New English Library
covers, where there was no
real need for it.

LEFT SECRET SCORPIO

Cover for book by Alan Burt Akers, DAW Books, 1975. Kirby: 'Primitive sacrifices for long-forgotten gods, hair raising escapes, adventures galore, this writing is in the wonderful tradition mastered by Edgar Rice Burroughs.'

SEWERS OF OBLIVION

Cover for a role playing game book by Michael A. Stackpole, Corgi, 1985. More doings in the murky underworld – lots of mist and vapours. A nicely dim dark world to seek for strange artifacts.

TRANCED THAUMATURGE AND DRAGON MAIDEN

Private work, 1984. This picture came from an unused idea for the first of Terry Pratchett's *Discworld* novels. Kirby finished it out of interest and followed it with a simpler version which later became useful as a book cover.

PRINCESS SALINDRA

Cover for a role playing game book by Stein & Stein, Corgi, 1984. One of a series by these authors which went under the collective heading *Wizards, Warriors* and *You*.

23

HUROK OF THE STONE AGE

Cover for book by Lin Carter, DAW Books, 1979. A satisfying commission because it gave Kirby a chance to indulge one of his favourite occupations of playing with scale. He loves hugeness of scale and the way it is created by contrasts. Here the eye falls first on the stone heads, then we notice the real dinosaurs looking tiny and insignificant below, then in the foreground we have the standard by which in the end we measure everything – the human figure in turn dwarfed by the dinosaurs.

GOLDEN SCORPIO

Cover for book by Alan Burt Akers, DAW Books, 1978.

25

DUELMASTER II
BLOOD VALLEY

Role playing game book cover, 1985. One of a matching pair for separate halves of the game (see also page 12).

OPPOSITE PAGE
KROZAIR OF KREGAN

Cover for book by Alan Burt Akers, DAW Books, 1976. A dangerous world with traps and monsters to snare and thwart our hero. But, come what may, he battles on!

ERIC OF ZANTHODON

Cover for book by Lin Carter, DAW Books, 1981. At first this looks a pretty standard barbarian hero/drooping maiden scenario. However, the hero's constipated look of self importance is somewhat undermined when one notices what the maiden's right hand is about to do. The volcano becomes more poignant too.

DINOCOPTER IDYLL

Private work, 1982. While doing a short feature on him, Anglia Television wanted some shots of Kirby at work. Not wanting the world to see his most usual mode – crouched nose to canvas over the board in his 'cupboard', Kirby began a large-scale work which ended up as this.

SHATTERED REALM

Cover for a role playing game book, Corgi, 1985. A dark female
warrior, for a change, challenging wizardry and magic through the
various hazards of the game.

OPPOSITE PAGE
DRAGONSLAYER

Cover for a role playing game book by Stein & Stein, Corgi, 1984. This commission gave Kirby a long-awaited opportunity to paint a fire-breathing dragon. 'A lot of fun,' he says.

KNIGHT OF THE GOLDEN HELM

Cover for a role playing game book by Stein & Stein, Corgi, 1984. 'Giants have always held a fascination for me,' says Kirby, 'and I enjoy the problems of scale and of trying to suggest the unlikeliness of laying them low in face-to-face combat.'

TIGERSNAKE

Cover for a role playing game book by Stein & Stein, Corgi, 1984. A bizarre creature in the world of tunnels and caverns, blocking progress to a hall full of gold no doubt!

GIANT OF SKULL CASTLE

Cover for a role playing game book by Stein & Stein, Corgi, 1984. Another opportunity for Kirby to paint a favourite theme.

33

SWORDSHIPS OF SCORPIO

Cover for book by Alan Burt Akers, DAW Books, 1975. Here we see the Kirby trolls which have recently resurfaced on the covers of some of Terry Pratchett's *Discworld* novels. Kirby felt a little uneasy about this even though it was only his own idea that he was stealing, but they did fit perfectly.

ALDAIR IN ALBION

Cover for book by Neal Barrett Jr, Daw Books, 1975. The first of a series of novels which appealed to Kirby because of their pure fantasy and happy contempt for possibility.

ALDAIR ACROSS THE MISTY SEA

Cover for book by Neal Barrett Jr, DAW Books, 1975. Kirby: 'This author peoples his books with alien creatures much to my taste. I used to get most of his books when I was working with Don Wollheim of DAW Books.'

CHAPTER TWO

MAGIC ENTERTAINMENTS

A slight handicap Josh Kirby suffers as an illustrator is the time he spends on his pictures, four to six weeks being quite common for a good cover with the depth of detail of, say, *The Majipoor Chronicles* at the start of this book (page 5). By fine art standards this is a manic pace but not in publishing where most of his competitors would allow only a week or two.

His pace is a secret Kirby has often kept from art directors for fear of frightening them away. One device for doing so is starting work on a picture before the rough has been approved. This usually works because more often than not his first idea is accepted (a change from the beginning when he had to submit six or seven alternatives). However, it sometimes means ending up with two versions of a painting. Does he mind this? 'Not particularly. The effort isn't wasted because I have two pictures instead of one.'

Doing more than one version of a theme is a common Kirby practice anyway when time permits, as is painting any other scenes that come to mind when working on a commission, just to explore the subject. If it was not for this pace and his extra-professional excursions, Kirby supposes he would be quite well off. But he has no plans to change his habits because ultimately he remains more interested in painting than money, which he has little enough time to spend as it is.

Although at one time he might have been equally tempted by the fine art road, the great bonus for Kirby in illustration is that you get to stretch your imagination and skill to the limits and can then hang the result up for as long as you like. Your brainchildren go out into the world without ever leaving home – no having to deliver them in trust to complete strangers who happen to walk in off the street with enough money. In an imperfect world it is not a bad deal.

Innocent happiness, that is what gets lost so soon in a cynical world, and is the spirit Kirby tries to capture in this work. Does he have any children of his own? 'No. It's probably just as well. I think they are delightful little creatures but I wouldn't know what to do with one. All that setting of standards, I would find it rather hard I think.'

The pictures in this chapter are all pretty light hearted. Does Kirby think they are as significant as his others? 'Sometimes I wonder if they are, but I work on them as seriously as any other kind of picture. And humour can be quite profound, you know. Take Terry Pratchett – his books are not only hilarious but have quite deep strands of science and philosophy. Also Bruegel could be quite droll at times – pricking the balloons of people's dignity. Why not?'

The mood of these pictures is that of the lighter fairy tales we read as children. Here we have dragons and maidens, wizards and witches, trolls, dwarves and goblins and all the rest, but we know everything will turn out all right in the end (except for those who don't deserve it). Their mood is basically frivolous but, as Kirby says, why not? Frivolity may need to know some bounds but a more common problem among adults is having had it strangled almost to death somewhere along the line. It could even be argued (in the early hours of the morning over one's nth Scotch) that lack of frivolity is the prime cause of mid-life crises – it's all that pent-up irresponsibility striking back at last. But that would be to start taking it too seriously and would probably only lead to the bottle of Scotch being finished off and a tremendous hangover in the morning.

A MALADY OF MAGICKS

Cover for book by Craig Shaw Gardner, Headline, 1987. This book was the first of a trilogy in which a permanently sneezing wizard goes in quest of a cure with his assistant because the sneezing interferes with his spells.

BRIDE OF THE SLIME MONSTER

Cover for a book by Craig Shaw Gardner,
Headline, 1989. Part of a trilogy in which
the characters are trapped in a dimension
of B-movies (the cineverse) constantly
flipping from one to another with the help
of a magic ring, out of a cereal packet.

THE WITCHES OF KARRES

Cover for a book by James Schmitz,
Gollancz Paperbacks, 1988. Kirby: 'A
Golden Age writer. This is an early
humorous science fiction work on
an epic scale. I enjoyed reading the
book very much.'

1998

Cover for a book, Sphere, 1986. This was commissioned while the book was still in progress, so Kirby had to work from the radio scripts on which it was based. This was less difficult than it might have been because it so happened that he had heard the programmes first time round.

A DIFFICULTY WITH DWARVES

Cover for a book by Craig Shaw Gardner, Headline, 1988. This is part of a second trilogy that followed the adventures befalling the wizard's apprentice in trying to find a cure for the sneeze. This had proved incurable throughout the first three books.

WINGS

Cover for a book by
Terry Pratchett, Corgi/Doubleday,
1990. The book's original title was
Astronauts (to match *Truckers* and
Diggers) but Pratchett changed his
mind after seeing the cover. The story
is about some gnomes who live in a
department store which they believe
to be the whole world.

A MULTITUDE OF MONSTERS

Cover for a book by Craig Shaw
Gardner, Headline, 1988. The second
of a trilogy featuring a wizard in a flying
shoe. A slight liberty was taken with
scale because in the book the shoe is
so large that the wizard has to peep
out through the eye holes and hence
could not be seen. For the Griffin's
claws Kirby made a compromise
between the two main schools of
thought in Griffinology, one claiming
they are eagle's claws, the other lion's.

STRATA

Cover for a book by Terry Pratchett, 1988. This was a pre-*Discworld* novel that was nonetheless full of the promise realized in the *Discworld* series.

A NIGHT IN THE NETHERHELLS

Cover for a book by Craig Shaw Gardner, Headline, 1988. This is the final part of the first trilogy, and involves much activity in the hellish regions looking for a sneezing cure.

AN EXCESS OF ENCHANTMENTS

Cover for book by Craig Shaw Gardner, Headline, 1989. Kirby enjoys illustrating this American author's light fantasies because of their richness in his favourite material – giants, gnomes, wizards etc. Most of the creatures which appear are taken from the story but Kirby sometimes throws in a few of his own.

THE BRENTFORD TRILOGY

Cover for a book by
Robert Rankin, Abacus, 1988.
Kirby: 'I had to illustrate three
novels in one cover here, so I
decided to represent the overall
theme as the flying swan. This is
also the name of the pub in all
three books. I have represented
episodes from the three books
on the back of the swan.'

A DISAGREEMENT WITH DEATH

Cover for book by Craig Shaw Gardner, Headline, 1989.
This is the last of the trilogy in which a cure for sneezing is
finally discovered!

DEMON BLUES

Cover for a book by Esther Freisner, Sphere,
1990. Fun and games with the supernatural in
an American university and the desert.

TRUCKERS

Cover for a book by Terry Pratchett, Corgi/Doubleday, 1989. The first of a children's trilogy about gnomes that live under the floorboards in a big department store.

SLAVES OF THE VOLCANO GOD

Cover for a book by Craig Shaw Gardner, Headline, 1989. Another of the *Cineverse* trilogy. Here the hero is being rapidly translocated with the aid of his Captain Crusader ring.

OPPOSITE PAGE

PUCKLE VERSUS IRON

Postcard, Clouded Tiger Cards, 1981. This work was commissioned by an author for a manuscript yet to be submitted to publishers, the idea being to whet their appetites for the story. For whatever reason the stratagem failed because, as far as Kirby knows, the book was never published. A problem with the steam engine was finding reference material for the specific model mentioned in the story. In the end some imagination needed to be applied to pictures of Stephenson's Rocket.

DIGGERS

Cover for a book by Terry Pratchett, Corgi/Doubleday, 1989. The gnomes are exiled after the big store burns down and get involved in high jinks at the quarry where they hide out.

THE SPROUTS OF WRATH

Cover for a book by Robert Rankin, Abacus, 1988. Nefarious doings at the gas works.

THE DARK SIDE OF THE SUN

Cover for a book by Terry Pratchett. Corgi, 1988. One of Pratchett's early straight science fiction novels. It was re-issued with this new cover as a result of the interest created by the *Discworld* novels.

CHAPTER THREE

VOYAGE OF THE AYEGUY

This project can fairly be called Josh Kirby's *magnum opus*. It did not start out that way. In fact, it was not until about the third of the series that he realized it was one and he was clutching the thread of some new theme. This is quite a common experience for Kirby and one of the side effects of letting intuition have its head. Ideas build in his work almost of their own accord, developing organically into something new and surprising without him being aware of it.

As far as he can remember, what started it all was the suggestion by a poster company interested in his work that he paint a kind of intergalactic zoo. This resulted in *Adoration of the Imag* (a pun on magi). Next probably came *Arrival of the Ark* in which the only link he was aware of was a strong likeness between the aliens in them. On the third picture a thread emerged which led into several others before anything like a clear theme was apparent.

In 1979 the project was accelerated by another for Schanes and Schanes of California – that of publishing a limited edition portfolio of six Kirby paintings. This concentrated his attention and by the following year when it was published in San Diego the *Voyage* had a clear outline. Asked for some captions for the pictures Kirby protested that he was no writer, but ended up having to do them anyway. At the time he and everyone else were pleased with the results but now he is not so sure. A direct result of the portfolio was the commissioning of some covers in a similar style for Robert Silverberg's *Lord Valentine* trilogy. Well, it was not intended as a trilogy but that was how it turned out.

The theme is plainly a biblical one transposed to the realm of science fiction, which Kirby feels is only fitting since in his life the Church he might once have looked to for employment has been replaced by science fiction publishers. Is he at heart a religious painter then? 'What I want is to tackle the great spiritual themes artists have always tackled down the ages using the imagery of their patrons, the Church. When working on the *Ayeguy* paintings I feel I am doing the same.'

Mention of the Church and Bruegel is common when Kirby's talk touches the tangled relationship of art and finance. Plainly the lack of such patronage in the modern world is a lingering, if slight, grievance. Perhaps it is not by complete accident that he lives in a former rectory in the shadow of its church. But how many plausible excuses would he have been able to invent for squeezing his luscious ladies into altarpieces?

The style of these paintings has on a couple of occasions been compared with Richard Dadd, the unfortunate nineteenth-century painter who ended up in Broadmoor for murdering his even more unfortunate father in a fit of paranoia. Kirby finds this flattering because he loves and admires Dadd's best work, but he has never been aware of any influence.

The *Ayeguy* series is Kirby's ideal of how science fiction should be. But what does he feel about current and recent trends in practice? Does he, for example, like the new *Star Trek* television series? 'I'm afraid I haven't been able to get addicted to it. I could never miss an episode of the original series but this one just has not hooked me. The sets and special effects are obviously much better, but in a way the tackiness of the scenery was part of the charm of the original.'

Kirby's main criticism of the new series is that it tries too hard to reflect the current, fashionable values of society. For instance, the unnatural care with which the gender and colour of the crew have been balanced. To him it seems far too calculated a basis for a good story. Also he objects to issues like the equality of men and women working their way into the plot. Matters like that should just be self-evident, he says, instead of being openly argued out in fashionable terms which will be dreadfully dated in ten years.

ADORATION OF THE IMAG

Portfolio piece, poster, 1977. Homage from the elder Imag, offering the urn cask forged in pure irridium flame to rare fiecite, filled to the oricle with canst vapour, to lull all Imag and alien minds to forget what was, is and will be. The Vapour of Loms' forgotten worlds, the place of the Imag's longed-for oblivion . . . Crysines, Lawmaths, Longrills swarm and jostle for a sight of the tall stranger. All wonder at his glittering head – now clear, now glinting in the sun's light. The sun striking sparks off it like Zlone at his anvil as he casts his gaze over the shifting throng. What a strange name has this traveller of the void. The Imag struggle with their vocal valves to form 'Jay Zuzz' on the thin mercurial air. He is ours, he says.

GARDEN OF UNEARTHLY DELIGHTS

Private work, 1981. A vision of the home planet of Jay Zuzz,
the drama's central figure.

Go Civilise the Savage Planets

Private work, 1982. The command is given!

Arrival of the Ark

Portfolio piece, 1979. Planetfall. The Ark disgorging men and machines to make ready the fulfilment of the Imag, who scurry and hop, laze and leap in their friendly efforts to make the Ayeguy welcome. No shadow falls here. No hint of the treachery to come. 'All hail the Mothership of the Ayeguy!' . . . the flute intones with a jaunty air. Hoists and hawsers, pulleys and whelps grind, lash and hiss. As the Imag secure the great vessel unscathed by the meteor showers, unscathed by the mighty pull of time warps, with their fine spun threads, confident that all is well when the strange travellers' voyager is securely lashed and linked with the magnetic horns of Dangra.

DEATH OF A SPACEMAN I

Portfolio piece, 1980. Jay Zuzz on the Kanzon treelith, pinned and spiked till he moves no more. The Imag grieve and bicker – on the one hand for his loss and on the other for who shall have what of his unearthly artefacts, bit by bit unclasped from his lifeless form. The dice game will decide, winner take all. Zang-ray ready in the rough-hewn lobcart. The Ark has left, perhaps never to return. A Zangth intoned a plaintive air. The Ayeguy's prime directive in shattered fragments, hazy dustmotes, at the Kanzon treelith's root. Has the Mothership deserted the son of the Overlord?

DEATH OF A SPACEMAN II

Private work, 1984. The spaceman is taken down from the treelith to be ceremoniously entombed.

DEPOSITION

Portfolio piece, 1980. Jay Zuzz being lowered with care from the Kanzon treelith. Stout Zanon takes his deadweight as he is eased onto the waiting cerum carriage. This is seen only on the great occasions of grief or loss, where recompense is thought to be due. The Imag have brought Sensor the robot to clear their minds of the Vapours of Loth, to help them remember their actions, actions that can break what they value most. The maidens of the inland seas of Varvor look where they will, when the langours of Loth-mist lessen.

ENTOMBMENT I

Private work, 1983.
Jay Zuzz is lowered
into the tomb.

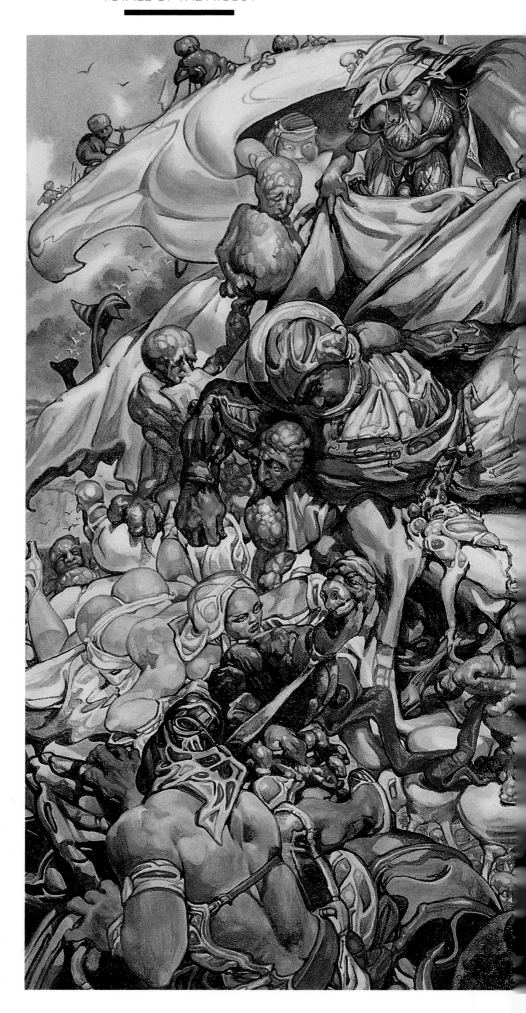

PREVIOUS SPREAD
ENTOMBMENT II
Private work, 1984.
Another version of
Jay Zuzz's interment.

RESURRECTION

Private work, 1981. Jay Zuzz
bursts triumphantly through the
tomb shell. He lives!

ASCENSION

Portfolio piece, 1980. The Mothership returns, activates the light guidance ascender beam to boost Jay's rover pack. Jay's suit medicure unit has renewed vital fluids, healed broken fibres, restored pulsing tissue. Jay lives once more and feels the suction of the antigrav as he nears the sanctuary of the Ark. Oil smooth limbs, silk metal-skinned robots hiss and glide on roller feet, slightly out of phase as the fringe of the antigrav radiation numbs their circuits. A soft maiden of Varvor has thoughts of times that might have been. Old bones prompt an elder to the vague consciousness of unheard-of happenings, never again to be known, now gone, lost among the receding multitudes of milliseconds . . .

PREVIOUS SPREAD

DEPARTURE

Private work later used on the cover of Robert Silverberg's *To Open the Sky*, Sphere Books, 1979. The Mothership of the Ayeguy provisioned and ready to blast across the vastness of the nether reaches of space. The order emblazoned and vivid in the crew's minds: 'Go civilize the savage planets;' The eerie whine of the piper's theme weaves a strange backcloth with counter melodies sensuously strummed by the maidens of Loth and Leveth. Jay Zuzz dreams of other worlds, lush meadows with emerald seas . . . His mind being drawn by the dulcet soothing strains borne on the balmy yet expectant air to his control console high above the thronging multitudes of the Ayeguy. Robots, men, machines, crymorphs, zanzers converge with but a single purpose at the airlocks of the Ark, each duty done to ensure safe passage through the blazing suns and mist banks of the spinning rocks, to alien worlds.

AFTER IMAGE

74

Private work, 1976. A precursor to the *Voyage of the Ayeguy* series.

CHAPTER FOUR

MAIDENS AND MONSTERS

This double series sprang from Josh Kirby's impatience with his usual rate of producing finished pictures. What he needed, and found, was a format simple enough to allow rapid completion while allowing room for improvisation. Two slightly different approaches were taken but all the pictures were painted at about the same time in 1982.

The first of the 'giant' series was prompted by someone asking to buy a Kirby painting. Not having any to hand that he wanted to part with, Kirby produced a new one which of course he was just as reluctant to sell when it came to the point. The rest of the series were done purely for his own pleasure, all but the final two in which the tale of the first was more or less repeated. What was the attraction of the theme? 'Well, I suppose it's archetypal isn't it? Fairy-tale stuff – beauty and the beast. You know, the frog the girl is sitting on is really a prince. And the giants, they are of course the brute side of human nature magnified to grotesque proportions against the poor little nymphets.'

The giant pictures can be looked at in two ways. From one angle we see how crude and uncontrollable male lust can be in the face of unattainable beauty. From the other we see a virgin's exaggerated fear of the unknown (and very successful defence of her honour by the look of it). For Kirby the giants are just as much princes under a spell as the frog, they just do not get the option of a kiss. There is some message here about the danger of uncontrolled natural urges – but pathos, too, in the giant we see helplessly adoring Selphine in her sleep.

While painting the pictures Kirby felt very much that he was dramatizing some basic sexual drama; this is plain enough as it takes shape on the canvas but less easy to capture in words. And this, Kirby feels, is how it should be. Giving shape to ideas is his prime aim –

analysis comes later, if at all. To him it is a secondary exercise that usually misses the point of his paintings, entertaining at times but not really necessary. 'Sometimes it is better not to know everything,' he says. 'Take King Arthur and all the books there are about him. Would we be better off if someone proved once and for all exactly who he was and what he did?'

Has Kirby ever been criticized by feminists for his portrayal of women? He certainly has. 'Sometimes I feel expected to apologize for being a man and having male urges.' The most strident of such attacks genuinely alarm him, reminiscent as they are of religious fanaticism.

Kirby does not mind anyone not liking his work and is quite prepared to enter friendly discussions about it, but in the end he feels it absurd that anyone should expect him to analyze his painting while he is in the middle of doing it 'because it's like trying to analyze what you are doing in the middle of a raging river. Fighting for your life sometimes, that's what art feels like. There's no time for notebooks. You don't wonder about the reality of the next rock that's rushing towards you, the buffeting of the water. Because it's called imagination people think it is unreal, but it is real when you are there. You cannot argue it away, it is as real as this world.' More so, perhaps, in Kirby's case as he spends more time there.

Because he means no harm to anyone he sees no reason why he should not paint anything that pleases him. And if it then goes on to please others something has been communicated to the world that it did not know before, so he is fulfilling his role as an artist. 'Paintings are just paintings,' he says. 'When I paint I do not want to be distracted by arguments that have nothing to do with the story. All I want is to paint the images that come into my mind.'

SELPHINE ATTACKS
Private work, 1982. Kirby: 'The idea that apparently frail and beautiful maidens can overcome such odds is intriguing to me.'

SELPHINE VICTORIOUS
Private work, 1982.
The giant laid low!

SELPHINE VICTOR
Private work, 1982. Selphine
highly satisfied after her triumph.

SELPHINE VANQUISHER
Private work, 1982. Selphine
showing how it's done.

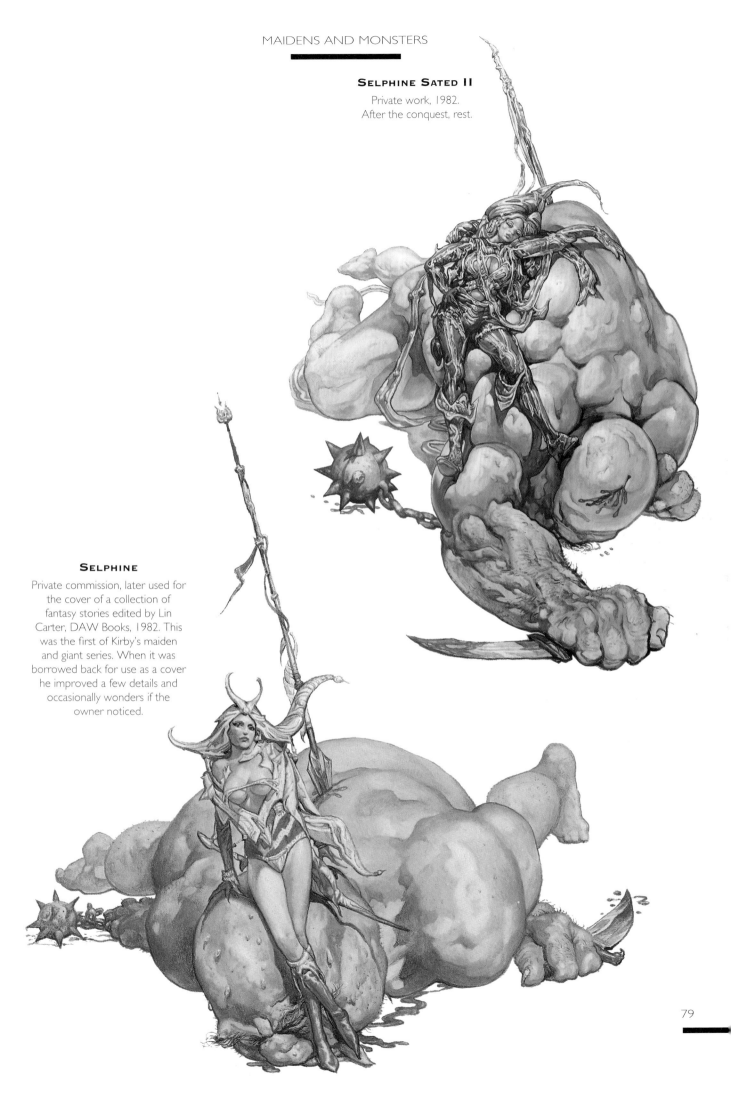

SELPHINE SATED II
Private work, 1982.
After the conquest, rest.

SELPHINE
Private commission, later used for the cover of a collection of fantasy stories edited by Lin Carter, DAW Books, 1982. This was the first of Kirby's maiden and giant series. When it was borrowed back for use as a cover he improved a few details and occasionally wonders if the owner noticed.

SELPHINE SATED

Private work, 1982.
Selphine takes an estimate
of the giant's girth.

SELPHINE AND ONE-EYE

Private work, 1982.
This is the biggest one
she has downed yet!

SELPHINE AND TROPHY
Private work, 1982.
She's feeling pretty confident
at this giant-killing lark.

THRENODY
Private work, 1982.
A sad lament to mark
a sad demise.

81

KALINDA AND SERPENT

Private work, 1982.
Kalinda relaxes with her
swamp companion.

DRAGARA AND SPORT

Private work, 1982.
Dragara has tamed
this immature specimen
once and for all.

PRINCESS ON FROG

Private work, 1982.
In folklore princesses
and frogs have long
been associated

SELPHINE ADORED
Private work, 1982.
Although caught napping,
Selphine fortunately has
the giant entranced.

SELPHINE VANQUISHED
Private work, 1982.
Selphine has a tricky
problem here.

CHAPTER FIVE

SWORD AND SORCERY

To Kirby the main attraction of fantasy is the wealth of wild and colourful imagery to be called on. And what makes it even better is the usual lack of need for any reference material (the search for which used to drive him mad in his days as a general illustrator), because the only place it is to be found is in the imagination.

In theory he has no objection to the use of photographic references, a common practice among even fantasy artists. It is just that he finds them a cramp on the imagination. 'You can never find pictures of models in quite the right position and so on. In fantasy I only use references if something needs to be recognized – a Morris Minor, say, or a tiger. If I have to be realistic I prefer to use the actual thing as a model. Photographs are a last resort, often line drawings are more useful. Sometimes I use photographs in a general way. Arnold Schwarzenegger for instance; I used some pictures of him to see how all those bulging muscles and veins fit together. They weren't in the required pose, though. Usually I use myself as a model for awkward hand positions and so on.'

The pictures in this chapter could be described as primal fantasy in which the struggle to keep a head on one's shoulders leaves little room for laughs. Most of them were for the covers of role playing game books, which raises a slight problem for the illustrator as the various possible stories have been finely chopped and thoroughly shuffled together. It is almost necessary to play the game to find a scene to illustrate.

The more usual procedure is for Kirby to be given a book to read. In doing so he makes 'scribbles' whenever he comes to an illustratable scene, sometimes ending with a great mound of them, each with a page number. (Most scenes would just vanish if he failed to do this because they only materialize within the 'feel' of the book.) Then he sifts through the pile until he finds what he needs. Occasionally Kirby does simply read

through a book and then look for some image to sum it up, but only when there is a specific reason for doing so.

By far the trickiest problem, though, is how to illustrate a book from no more than a publisher's précis of the story, an increasing practice which Kirby suspects has crept over from the film industry where advance publicity has been raised to a fine art. The last thing any self-respecting précis contains is description of any length, so how is an artist supposed to come up with a picture? Divine inspiration is often the only recourse but cannot always be relied on. Apart from the inevitable mistakes and confusion this practice causes, Kirby feels a little uneasy about its honesty.

The storyboard series of pictures was commissioned for a film proposal which, as far as he knows, never took off. They are far more detailed than is usual for film, probably to encourage potential backers, and so far it is the only time he has done such work.

How does Kirby rate these sword and sorcery pictures compared with other areas of his work? 'I find it hard to evaluate my own paintings. Sometimes I am embarrassed by things other people turn out to like, sometimes it is the other way round. When I had a set of postcards made I couldn't bear some of the paintings they chose, but on seeing them in print I actually got to like one or two. Some still make me uncomfortable, but then I spend my life feeling uncomfortable about all manner of things. You just have to put up with it.

'Life is all a mystery to me, you know. It's all science fiction when you think about it – us glued here by gravity to a ball spinning through space, sitting here in this 400-year old house made basically of wood and unbaked mud. Consider the first rector here as an incipient astronaut waiting in the living quarters across the meadow from the petrified spaceship sitting on its launching pad, where weekly telepathic 'communals' attempted to generate sufficient prayer-power for blast-off. It's all unreal, isn't it?'

MISTY COMBAT

Film storyboard, 1984. In the twilight a warrior wields a star-studded mace against the shield of the female warrior.

IN THE ROCKPOOL

Film storyboard, 1984. The Gremlins soon become aware of the Prince and the Siren laying helplessly at the base of the empty rock pool.

DARK TOWER

Film storyboard, 1984. In the castle courtyard the people gasp in amazement as the darkness is dispelled by a cascade of spectral light.

GREMLINS ON THE ROCK STAIR

Film storyboard, 1984. Within the cliff thousands of narrow steps have been sculpted . . . with incredible speed the Gremlins carry the struggling Siren upwards towards the Dark Tower.

OPPOSITE PAGE
SNAKEPIT

Film storyboard, 1984. High in the Inner Chamber the final desperate drama unfolds.

CITY OF TERRORS

Cover for a role playing game book by Michael A. Stackpole, Corgi, 1985. Yet another hero faced with unequal odds in the underworld.

MISTY WOOD

Cover for a role playing game book by Michael A. Stackpole, Corgi, 1985. A many-headed serpent meeting its match.

NAKED DOOM

Cover for a role playing game book by Ken St Andre, Corgi, 1985. Fully accoutred warrior hero setting forth on his quest.

89

TUNNELS AND TROLLS RULE BOOK

Role playing game book cover, 1985. Our hero throws a bolt at the treasure guardian.

BEYOND THE SILVERED PLAIN

Cover for a role playing game book by Ken St Andre, Corgi, 1985. Fighting his way out of a tight spot.

OPPOSITE PAGE

BLUE FROG TAVERN

Cover for a role playing game book by Michael A. Stackpole, Corgi, 1985. Slaying the wood dragon.

CHAPTER SIX

DEMONS AND WHIMSY

In many ways Josh Kirby would have preferred this book to appear without any text beyond perhaps picture titles. Really he feels that everything important he has to say has been expressed in paint. The past, his opinions and way of life seem to him almost irrelevant to the work.

'The trouble' he says, 'with living an intense inner life is that there is not much to show for it apart from paintings, there is not much to talk about. If you watched an artist at work for a hundred years it would not be very entertaining, would it? All you see is someone sitting in a room scratching his ear from time to time. Crossing his legs. There is not much action to see because it all takes place in the mind and on canvas. My Rambo leaps are a millimetre long – the stroke of a brush. I paint most of the time and while painting I do not think in words about what I am doing, the language is visual, so there is not much left to talk about, is there?'

Fighting off a sudden terrifying vision of blank pages, your reporter improvises a rapid justification of his existence which Kirby digests thoughtfully. Then, with only a faint sigh of resignation he shoulders the burden of distraction like a true professional. The next question is – where to pick up the thread . . ?

Does he listen to music while painting? 'Never, because it completely confuses my thinking. It is creative on the same level I suppose. But I listen to Radio 4 all the time, all day long. Because it is all speech there is no distraction. Sometimes my painting interferes with the programmes, I get so caught up in the work I hear nothing for hours, but never the other way round.'

Hmm. Dead end. Oh yes, that's where we were heading – Terry Pratchett and Kirby's covers for the *Discworld* novels which make up the bulk of this chapter and have earned him the rare distinction for an illustrator (rarer even than having his name appear in anything other than microscopic print in the most obscure corner of the book) of having his name

recognised and associated with his work. The chiming of their imaginations is obvious but how did Kirby come to get the job in the first place?

It is all a bit of a mystery, it seems. Kirby has no idea at all why he was offered *The Colour of Magic*, the first of the series whose success could hardly have been predicted. He had done science fiction covers for Corgi before, but many years earlier and occasional contacts in between had never come to anything. Also, he was not particularly well known in England as a science fiction illustrator because for a long time his work was only published in the US. 'It was all very puzzling, the way it came from nowhere and worked so well,' he says. Whatever the reason, it happened and Kirby has provided covers for all of Terry Pratchett's books since, including *Eric*, a *Discworld* tale which he also fully illustrated throughout.

Their happy collaboration does not mean they always agree on every detail. For instance, Pratchett's own view of his witches is that they are rather homely looking females but Kirby could not help painting them the way he felt witches should look. Next time they were called for he tried harder to compromise, but not because of any undue pressure. It is a loose collaboration and he is left pretty much to his own interpretations.

What are the *Discworld* books about? Kirby: 'They are personified by a galloping piece of luggage, malevolent yet "handy", supplying all good things to its current owner (including lethal defence). Humour and shrewd social comment and airy philosophy and droll science thread their way through the frantic, even manic, efforts of the inhabitants of the Discworld to survive. Here we have a collision of half-baked spells and the elbowing aside of other incompetents to reach the top of the pile, just as the Discworld is precariously balanced on top of its own cosmic pile – turtle, elephants and all! Here perhaps we have Bruegel in literary form.'

THE TOWER OF SCREAMING DEATH
Computer game box top, Games Workshop Ltd, 1987. Kirby never heard if this was published as a box top, though it was used by the same company for a non-computer game called *Warhammer.*

WYRD SISTERS

Cover for book by Terry
Pratchett, Gollancz/Corgi, 1988.
Kirby: 'Curiously enough this
was inspired by Piero dela
Francesca's painting of Christ
rising from the tomb in glory.'

GUARDS! GUARDS!

Cover for book by Terry Pratchett, Gollancz/Corgi, 1989. This featured the first dragon in the *Discworld* series.

DISCWORLD

Illustration for book by Terry Pratchett, Gollancz, 1990. Kirby wanted to paint an overview of the Discworld for a while before the *Eric* project gave him the chance by calling for full-page illustrations throughout and removed the usual typographical constraints on covers. This picture originally had a large white area on the left for text, but Kirby later painted it in.

MOVING PICTURES

Cover for book by Terry Pratchett, Gollancz/Corgi, 1990. The original title of this book was *Hurrah for Hollywood*. Kirby's original idea for the cover (which he went ahead and painted while waiting for the publisher's approval) was to have the main elements of the left and right halves the other way round. So now he has both.

THE OTHER SINBAD

Cover for a book by Craig Shaw Gardner, Headline, 1990. This is an instance of where divine inspiration in large measures is called for because all Kirby had to work on was a letter from the author. Where will it all end?

ROYAL CHAOS

Cover for a book by Dan McGirt, Pan, 1990. For this sequel to *Jason Cosmo*, Kirby worked from a précis of the story. The horse in the picture was a lucky guess.

99

PREVIOUS SPREAD
EQUAL RITES

Cover for book by Terry Pratchett, Corgi, 1986. At this point Kirby did not yet know Pratchett personally and so only discovered that they had a completely different perception of witches when the painting was finished. Although they debated the point, no changes in the picture were called for.

JASON COSMO

Cover for a book by Dan McGirt, Pan, 1990. Kirby: 'The plot of this book was rather like a series of role playing games with numerous trolls and griffins and the like – lots of scope!'

THE COLOUR OF MAGIC

Cover for book by Terry Pratchett, Corgi, 1984. The first of Kirby's *Discworld* covers is also the only watercolour. The rest of the series, as with almost all his work, are oil paintings. It was also the only watercolour Kirby had done for years. The reason was simply that it seemed a shame not to use up a piece of particularly fine, but now discontinued, watercolour board that was lying around.

MORT

Cover for book by Terry Pratchett, Gollancz/Corgi, 1987. In this story Death takes on an apprentice. Gollancz also began publishing a hardback edition before its paperback launch.

PYRAMIDS

Cover for book by Terry
Pratchett, Gollancz/Corgi, 1989.
This is the first time the Trojan
horse equivalent appears in the
Discworld. Also appearing is
the evil-minded camel that can
pick off flies with a
well-aimed jet!

FOLLOWING SPREAD

**THE FOUR DEADLY
RIDERS: CHAOS, LUST,
HATE & MADNESS**

Private commission, 1981. The
theme of this painting was
suggested by the American
who commissioned it and is a
sort of hybrid of the Seven
Deadly Sins and the Four
Horsemen of the Apocalypse.
Exactly how and why the seven
were whittled down to four,
Kirby is not sure but it seemed
a fair enough challenge to paint.
As time permits, he is currently
working on a much larger
version for himself which is 6 ×
4ft (180 × 120cm).

105

HERE BE DEMONS

Cover for a book by
Esther Freisner, Sphere, 1989.
The first of a trilogy. Demons and
succubi having fun in the desert
tempting a dessicated monk.

MORLOCK NIGHT

Cover for a book, DAW Books,
1979. The story was an H. G.
Wells pastiche in which the
Morlocks usurp the time machine
and come to London.

109

THE LIGHT FANTASTIC

Cover for book by Terry
Pratchett, Corgi, 1985. The
second of the *Discworld* series.
Kirby: 'I was glad to get another
Terry Pratchett as it wasn't
clear after *The Colour of Magic*
that there would be another of
his books for me to do.'

SOURCERY

Cover for book by Terry Pratchett. Gollancz/Corgi, 1988. This book featured the return by popular demand of the Luggage. We see the Luggage plummet from the heights of love to the pits of despair, then haul himself back to sanity again heroically – all without it saying a word or even blinking.

CHAPTER SEVEN

HITCHCOCK, POE AND HORROR

The idea of illustrating faces without losing their likeness was prompted by some French postcards of Napoleon whose face, on closer inspection, was composed of a number of cleverly arranged naked ladies. The ultimate inspiration for these was almost certainly Arcimboldi, whose portraits in fruit, vegetable, game or almost anything else that came to hand still have the power to startle after several centuries – but Kirby only discovered him later.

Ray Bradbury's *Illustrated Man* animated the idea and set off a series which includes portraits of Ray Bradbury, Forrest J. Ackerman, Clement Freud, Jack Kerouac, Edgar Allan Poe and Alfred Hitchcock. The Hitchcock heads were for a series of horror anthologies. Only one drew on the stories themselves for inspiration. For the rest Kirby just let his imagination roam.

Does Kirby like horror? What does he say to those who claim it is a backdoor to satanism and the like? 'I love it and can see no harm in it at all. These people confuse imagination and reality. Imagination does have its own reality, yes, but my bats and witches and things cannot get out of the picture. They are safely locked up in a realm of the imagination.

If I believed they were real, or that I was helping to make them real, I'd be terrified.

'Horror is also a legitimate theme for artists. Think of Goya and Hieronymous Bosch, did they not paint much the same scenes?' He finds it imaginatively interesting, that is all, and has all the normal revulsion for people who dabble seriously in witchcraft and satanism. 'In art it is attractive just because it is not real. Horror stories and fairytales have a lot in common, they both tap deep into the subconscious and consider the workings of dark forces, but they are unreal so can be as wild and terrifying as they like without doing any harm. Unlike, for example, video nasties which are something quite different.'

In the end Kirby cannot believe there is any harm in fantasies about witches and the like, no real horror, because he cannot believe any part of his own mind could be so 'occluded' that he could entertain them without knowing it. Would Hitchcock perhaps be a good illustration of this harmlessness, given the homely face he presented to the world? 'Hitchcock was in fact a bit too real for me. I was terrified by *Psycho*. Luckily showers hadn't been invented in England then.'

GET ME TO THE WAKE ON TIME
Book cover, Mayflower, 1973.
Kirby: 'Hitchcock always intrigued me – he has a fascinating face to play around with.'

EDGAR ALLAN POE
This is an example of Kirby's 'grand master' style of portrait painting, based on a daguerrotype, which Kirby loves, 1975.

STORIES TO BE READ WITH THE LIGHTS ON II

Book cover, Pan, 1973. The artist having fun with Hitchcock's head.

NOT FOR THE NERVOUS I

Book cover, Pan, 1974. This is the only case of Kirby illustrating Hitchcock's face with scenes from the stories in the anthology.

STORIES TO STAY AWAKE BY

Book cover, Pan, 1974. Kirby: 'Thought I'd have a mermaid in this one.'

NOT FOR THE NERVOUS

Book cover, Pan, 1973.

MONTH OF MYSTERY I

Book cover, Pan, 1972. This was the
first of the peopled Hitchcock heads.

MONTH OF MYSTERY II

Book cover, Pan, 1972. Kirby: 'I think
the chicken claw hand says it all.'

**STORIES TO BE READ
WITH THE LIGHTS ON I**

Book cover, Pan, 1975.

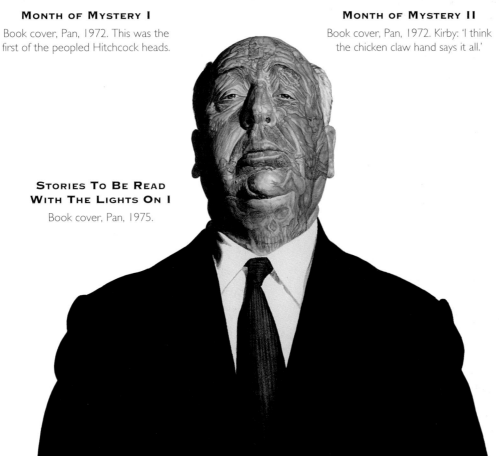

WEREWOLF

Editorial illustration for the magazine *Men Only*.
Also book cover, Pan, 1973. 'Something everyone should
try and paint at some point,' Kirby says.

SKULL WITH SHRIMP

Book cover for *Nightshades & Damnations*, Hodder & Stoughton, 1968. This was a still life (or perhaps death would be more appropriate) exercise for which Kirby arranged the items in his studio.

POE WITH SNAKES

Book cover, Sphere Books, 1972. Since Arcimboldi was the father of this kind of painting it seemed appropriate to apply it to Edgar Allan Poe, the father of horror writing. Based on another daguerrotype.

BRING OUT YOUR DEAD

Book cover, 1979. Only a detail of this picture was shown on the final cover because it was a rare instance of Kirby completely misreading his commission. There was an excuse in that he was given very little material to work from, but still his professional pride was a bit dented.

THE GRIM REAPER

Private work, 1974. Although painted purely for his own pleasure, this picture has since appeared on the covers of a couple of books, and as a postcard in 1981. 'A pleasant theme,' Kirby says.

ELEPHANT MAN

Cover for a book by Frederick Treeves, Ballantine, 1972. This portrait was based on an engraving of the actual man and was in fact commissioned for a quite separate book which in the end used a picture of *The Elephant Man* wearing his customary mask.

BIRDMAN

Private work, 1972. Kirby: 'Being born from an egg – it seemed an interesting idea, even if the wings didn't appear to be included in the deal.'

WITCH ON BAT

Book cover, Sphere, 1978.
This witch is well past
her prime.

MUMMY I

Postcard, Clouded Tiger Cards,
1981. This is one of a pair –
a daddy mummy. . .

THE WITCH

Book cover, Pan, 1975. People sometimes imagine Kirby's mind must be full of horrors but he has never felt this. It is just that when he visits the appropriate area of the imagination, horror is what he uncovers there.

MUMMY II

. . . and this is the mummy mummy! Private work, 1981.

123

CHAPTER EIGHT

ALIENS AND ANDROIDS

Although they alliterate pleasantly and often appear together in science fiction, aliens and androids seem almost opposite to Kirby. He enjoys painting both but for quite different reasons. 'Aliens are other life forms' he says, 'whereas androids are merely a more or less clumsy version of us.' In other words, a kind of substitute peasantry – biddable, unprotesting and cheap to run. Of course, as with other robots in real life it rarely works out like that, which is the attraction for Kirby. Half the fun of robots, he says, is their literal-mindedness and basic stupidity, whereas aliens have an inherent dignity.

Does he believe there really are weird creatures living out there on other planets? 'Of course' comes the surprised reply of one forced to defend the obvious. 'And life forms will have evolved in completely different ways to here on earth. That's what is so interesting – if you lived on another planet you would tend to copy whatever is going on around you, so bug-eyes and tentacles could be just as effective as anything we have.'

Kirby feels that on the whole aliens have had a bad press in earthly fiction and would love to see some real ones appear, finding it hard to believe they could be any more of a menace to the earth than humans are. A science fiction theory that appeals to him is that the earth began as a kind of galactic lunatic society.

Does he believe the spate of recent claims, particularly in the USA, of people being snatched up into spaceships for examination by aliens? 'I don't know enough about it, but it's strange how many people you meet who have seen strange lights and flying saucers with their own eyes, without it being considered a common thing.' It happened to him. One night while driving along with his wife they saw a dazzling silvery light in the sky ahead. Stopping to investigate, they suddenly felt so dreadful they had to get away.

To prove his point, your narrator owns up to an almost identical experience as a teenager walking home in the early hours of the morning, the only difference being that it was sheer panic that made me run. Kirby also once saw a large, smooth and featureless object hovering over Fleet Street in London, staying motionless for a long while over a growing crowd before moving away. The *Evening Standard* later explained it as a weather balloon and showed a picture of one deflated in a field. At the time Kirby swallowed this as easily as anyone else but looking back now he has doubts, wondering if maybe there are just a few too many weather balloons floating about. It seems hard to believe a balloon could be that big and stay so still for all that time in the free air.

When it comes to androids he prefers antique ones with lots of Victorian cogs and wheels. The more they have to resemble humans the less interesting he finds them. Because they are by definition human-like, androids embody and attract the whole range of human/machine conflicts and contrasts. Computers, like Hal in *2001*, have encroached on the android's territory but, given human vanity, it seems unlikely they will ever take over completely. Computers might offer a cerebral or spiritual challenge but in the end who envies the lot of a computer? You cannot go anywhere for a start, but to have a powerful, tireless, statuesque body that is almost indefinitely repairable and immune to pain and disease – that challenges us on a quite different but equally important level. Add to this body a brain that ticks smoothly and efficiently and is not subject to erratic impulses like asking the old hypochondriac down the road how he's feeling today, and the level of challenge rises. All that is then needed is some micro-micro-electronic wizardry to give that brain capacity enough for an illusion of self-purpose and awareness and we are in danger of being shown up on every level.

Behind the attraction of androids as slaves lies the fear that they will be just as likely to get ideas above their station as the peasants of old. Even knowing this, the lure is as irresistible in real life as in science fiction because at the heart of the human/machine contrast lies the answer, or at least part of the question of what is it that makes humans so weird – why don't we behave like any other animal on the planet?

STRESS PATTERN

Cover for a book by Neal Barrett Jr, DAW Books, 1974. One of Josh Kirby's favourite pictures in which there is a kind of pre-echo of his *Ayeguy* series.

HAVEN OF DARKNESS

Cover for a book by E. C. Tubb,
Arrow Books. Poster and
postcard, Clouded Tiger Cards,
1979. This is part of the *Dumarest*
series and is by an author who
used to appear regularly in
Authentic Science Fiction.

EYE OF THE ZODIAC

Cover for a book by E. C. Tubb,
Arrow Books. Poster and
postcard, Clouded Tiger Cards,
1979. Kirby: 'Levitating platforms
have always fascinated me.'

SPECTRUM OF A FORGOTTEN SUN

Cover of a book by E. C. Tubb,
Arrow Books, 1979. Impaling the
slavering beast.

ELOISE

Cover for a book by E. C. Tubb, Arrow Books. Postcard, Clouded
Tiger Cards, 1978. A dangerous future world where robots run amok.

BATTLEFIELD EARTH II

Cover for a book by L. Ron Hubbard, 1984. Over the years, Kirby has done quite a few covers for the founder of Scientology whom he rates as a very good science fiction writer, being punchy and fast and always delivering cliffhangers bang on time, although he is a bit too 'scientific' for Kirby's own taste, which tends more to the fantastically improbable.

THE HERO OF DOWNWAYS

Cover for a book by Michael G. Coney, DAW Books, 1973. A story in which everyone was living in a joyless, dank and dismal underground world.

MIDSUMMER CENTURY

Cover for a book by James Blish, DAW Books, 1973.

OPPOSITE PAGE
THE MIND BEHIND THE EYE

Cover for a book by Joseph Green, DAW Books, 1971. Another favourite of Kirby's because of the chance to play with scale.

THE WICKED CYBORG

Cover for a book by Ron Goulart, DAW Books, 1977. This is one of the earliest humorous science fiction covers painted by the artist.

SWAMPWORLD WEST

Cover for a book by Perry A. Chapdelaine, Elmfield, 1974.

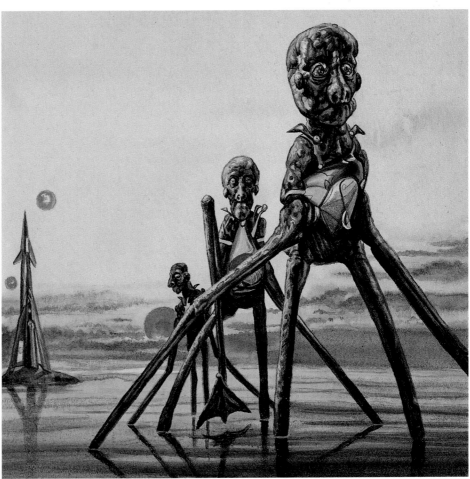

MINDBRIDGE

Cover for a book by Joe Haldeman, Orbit. Postcard, Clouded Tiger Cards, 1977.

THE ALIENS AMONGST US

Cover for a book by James White, Corgi, 1970. Usually when painting aliens Kirby is obliged to work within the parameters of the author's description, but in this case he had a free hand. Being rather fond of the creature he later decided to do a larger scale version, in fact his largest scale to date, the finished painting measuring over 8 × 6ft (240 × 180cm). The sky was painted with acrylics, the alien with oils and the picture has since appeared on the cover of *History of the Science Fiction Magazine, Part 2* by Michael Ashley.

THE LIGHT THAT NEVER WAS

Cover for a book by Lloyd Biggle Jr, Morley, 1974. These aliens were faithfully painted according to the descriptions in the book.

THE INTERPRETER

Cover for a book by Brian Aldiss, Four Square, 1966.
Kirby: 'This was painted to the same dimension as the
paperback – a bit too small but it was a habit of mine
in those days. I feel a fair amount of affection for this
sort of alien, bug-eyes and all!'

GALACTIC ODYSSEY

Cover for a book by Keith Laumer, Mayflower,
1974. A careful rendering of the verbal description
in the book.

135

TIME STORY

Cover for a book by Stuart Gordon, DAW Books, 1972. Kirby took the chance here to invent a strange building. The extreme redness of the picture was at the art director's insistence because he had fallen in love with a shade Kirby had used in the rough.

SPACE OPERA

Magazine illustration, *SF Monthly*, 1974.

137

THE DAY BEFORE TOMORROW

Cover for a book by Gerard Klein, DAW Books, 1972. A touch of Escher influence here.

THE ROBOT IN THE CLOSET

Cover for a book by Ron Goulart, DAW Books, 1980. Another of Ron Goulart's zany, madcap adventures.

OPPOSITE PAGE
OLE DOC METHUSELAH

Cover for a book by L. Ron Hubbard, DAW Books, 1972. This was for the reissue of an ancient piece of vintage science fiction by Hubbard, a series of short stories centred on this hero.

139

CALLING DR PATCHWORK

Cover for book by Ron Goulart,
DAW Books, 1980. Kirby: 'At this
time I was receiving each Ron
Goulart manuscript as it was
completed.'

A WHIFF OF MADNESS

Cover for a book by Ron Goulart,
DAW Books, 1981. This was Kirby's
second cover for Goulart in which he
adopted a much lighter style than the
first – *What's Become of Screwloose?*

HAIL HIBBLER

Cover for a book by Ron Goulart,
DAW Books, 1980. Kirby: 'I
thought I'd use a personified
rocket to sum up the wealth of
Hitler jokes in this book.'

HELLO LEMURIA HELLO
Cover for a book by Ron Goulart, DAW Books, 1981.

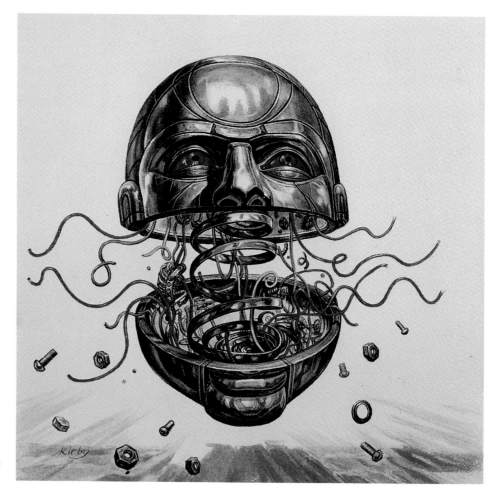

**WHAT'S BECOME OF
SCREWLOOSE?**

Cover for a book by Ron
Goulart, DAW Books. Postcard,
Clouded Tiger Cards, 1973. One
of the first Kirby covers for a
humorous writer and the first of
many for Ron Goulart. The later
pictures become more comical as
he gets to grips with his author.

BIG BANG

Cover for a book by Ron Goulart, DAW Books, 1982. They tried to blow up the moon in this one.

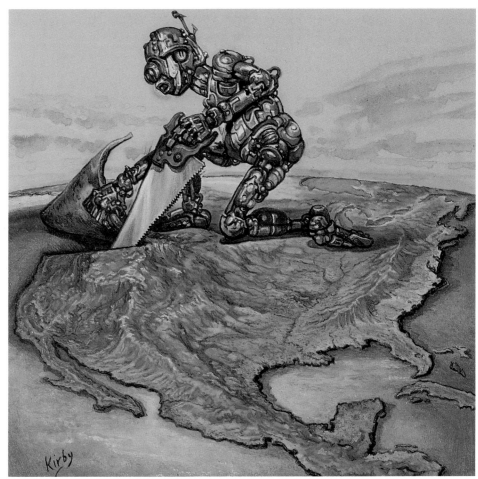

UPSIDE DOWNSIDE

Cover for a book by Ron Goulart, DAW Books, 1981. An illustration of the general feel of the book rather than any actual incident, not a common Kirby approach but one he is prepared to use when necessary.

143

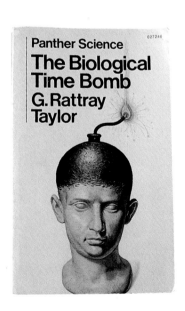

Panther Science
027246

**The Biological
Time Bomb**

G. Rattray
Taylor

GN7676 A CORGI BOOK

I can't sleep at night

zzzzzzzzzzzzzzzz Weird tales by Ray Bradbury
Robert Bloch, zz **August Derleth,** zz **William
Tenn** zz & others zzzEdited by Kurt Singer zzz

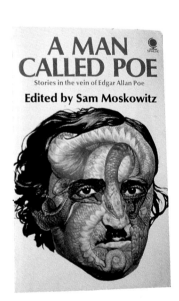

**A MAN
CALLED POE**

Stories in the vein of Edgar Allan Poe

Edited by Sam Moskowitz